LIGN SERIES / I

Borage Blue

Oliver Southall

XYLEM BOOKS 2019

LIGN SERIES

LS1   Oliver Southall, *Borage Blue*

Oliver Southall, *Borage Blue*
First published in 2019 by Xylem Books

ISBN: 978-1-9999718-8-5

Xylem Books is an imprint of Corbel Stone Press

I

II

Borage Blue

Why do precisely these objects which we behold make a world?

Henry David Thoreau

I

ON BORAGE

NOTES FOR AN IMPOSSIBLE POEM

'Borage', John Gerard writes in his *Herball*, 'Pliny calls Euphrosinum, because it maketh a man merry and joy-full'. And 'those of our time', he continues, 'do use [this herb] in sallads to exhilerate and make the mind glad.'

o

Such was the elevated position of Borage in the arsenal of vegetable correctives to darkness and introspection – a fame lavishly established in antiquity – that it is afforded pride of place in the emblematic frontispiece to Burton's *Anatomy of Melancholy*.

o

The importance of Borage to monastic herbalists is reflected in the binomial name of the plant, *Borago officinalis*. The genitive *officinalis* derives from 'officina' – the apothecary's storehouse of remedies for the corrupt body. And since that word comes, in turn, from the abbreviated roots of 'opus' and 'facere' (to work and to do), Borage is tied, by a chain of etymological connections, to both the cultural history of the body and the conceptual history of work.

Historically, the Latin 'opus' designated an operation quite distinct from mechanical toil or any merely life-enabling job – a field of endeavour, a vocation, in which the subject could achieve a transformative self-knowledge in the field of public action, the shared space of appearance. Crucial to the successful pursuit of such vocation was a practice of reflection known as 'otium'. Though often translated as 'leisure', this concept in fact denotes a period of withdrawal and contemplation in which, through reflection on past and future action, operational methods could be reflexively tuned so as to reconcile the demands of the end to be achieved with the need for the operant to maintain – and discover – in action, a unique and singular presence – a style.

o

Insofar as they can be assumed to have practiced a
Christianised 'otium', the work of the monastic herbalist
married self-care with a wider concern for the commu-
nity. Vital resource of courage and joy, Borage plays its
part in a ministry – or office – which is also testament
to an alternative historical conception of work: one in
which self-knowledge is achieved through a potentiating
interaction with other beings rather than in heroic acts of
creative externalisation, the rational transformation and
domination of nature.

o

The name Borage itself has a likely origin in the Latinate
word 'borra', meaning wool or hair. Hairiness, in fact,
is a significant characteristic of Borage and a crucial
component in the singular interaction of this herb with
light – an interaction which, perhaps counterintuitively,
contributes to the essentially cool and airy nature of the
plant: the holographic tendency which allows it, in bright
conditions, to tremble on the border of pure sensation.

o

Its petals in pellucid summer: a nerve-opening blue which proves the irreducibility of the affective to the material body.

o

As if to profess a faith that, in the practice of remember-
ing some blue, we might enter a region wider than any
geography, I look at the drab winter sky and imagine
Borage.

o

As part of its family (*Boraginaceae*), Borage can be considered a moment within a larger morphological becoming.

o

I admire two common features of the flowering growth of the Borages: the frequently plaited nature of the clustered flower-stalks and the retiring disposition of the flowers themselves – their tendency to hide themselves within a coat of sepals and to bow earthward, turned from the elevated passage of the human eye.

Both aspects – on the one hand, a delicate torsion and, on the other, a minimal indication of weight – help define a subtle equilibrium, a relation of imaginary forces, inwardly felt, which can only be described as unimpeachable pleasure.

o

In his work on elemental images of earth, air, fire and water, Gaston Bachelard transforms recurring literary images – the sense of airy lightness associated with dreams of flight, for example – into a set of analogies for the dynamics of affective self-relation: for a transformative inner awareness of freedom or constraint, joy and despair.

As with many arguments which propose a way of inter-preting the unruly transformations of feeling, Bachelard's vision initiates its own levitations of thought. Indeed, Bachelard's system, I imagine, might readily serve as the intellectual basis for a therapeutic practice both minimal in its use of resources and truly universal – a practice which, if comprehensively adopted, as in the form of a contagious aesthetic cult, would see a great and absurd transformation of society. Our profoundest need would be to find and consider those forms of matter – a rock, a cloud, a bird, a plant of Borage – which, quite aside from any reason, might initiate – seen, heard, touched – the feeling of spontaneous inner lightness associated with joy. And these flights of intensive introspection would prepare us for a truly generous and benevolent sociality – would spark a general exodus from the spiralling pattern of consumption and waste which fuels, each day, the murderous transformation of the earth.

o

When I caress a leaf of Borage, the sensation appears at
first to be laid out along the contact surface. With greater
focus, however, the same sensation cannot be limited
to this bounded haptic line; it assumes a somatic excess
which blurs the spatiality of sensation – it has, and has
not, this feeling, a spatial being.

o

To touch a leaf of Borage, to attend to that touch, is to be taken by the mystery of what is close at hand.

o

'Touch', Aristotle writes, 'is the primary sensation which belongs to all animals.' There is a touch preceding any particular touch, a touch appropriated to itself in the existence of what appears – of colour, of melody, line; it is from touch that thought takes form.

o

There is a projection of essential difference internal to each sensation that we experience: subject and object – distinct. This projective act is integral to the continuous emergence of consciousness from what, for reflection, appears as the blindness of unmediated feeling.

Within touch, however, there exists, always, a slippage from this projective movement. Touch, though it relies on bounded form, paradoxically obliterates externality, dissolves boundaries. And because it destroys that distance which permits reflection, touch can have no language of its own, is mute. It is, for this reason, the sense most closely associated with the practice of analogy – diverted through the visible, it urges a freely accumulating world of equivalences.

o

Viewed from below, a rotational symmetry between the petals of Borage and its long, rayed, sepals – five and five; blue, maroon. They appear to counter-pose one another as does a bright image to its retinal impression in the closed eye – a relation analogous to the groundless economy of form and feeling.

o

In the portion of organic matter defined as boraginaceous growth, blue and pink have been destined to enter a dynamic polarity – the one constantly in transition to the other.

o

Close-up, the Viper's Bugloss is as if a demonstration
of all that thrills in the precisely defined: rich blue
petals deep against the thin pink filaments, anthers. At
a distance, these same parts give the impression of a
blue-purple psychedelic smudge, haloed and uncontain-
able: ineffable contribution of the imperceptible to every
impression – as though a timbral aspect of the visible.

o

The *medium* of touch is the skin. The *organ* of touch, however, is an invisible membrane: the illimitable surface where sensitive life is emergent in matter.

If plants, capturing solar energy and ceaselessly transforming insensate matter into living being, can be considered the cosmogonic agents of such emergence, then perhaps the most apt analogy for the relation of touch to its world is the staggering, endlessly intricate surface of summer foliage. Like the surface of touch, this is an ontological, not merely spatial, surface; it is infinite, because it defines a universal limit and its emergence inverts the relationship of container and contained – such a surface is not 'in' the world, but establishes the existence of world within a new ontological horizon.

o

To touch a leaf of Borage: touch touching its condition, feeling its way to an analogy for its own being. A dizzying sacrament.

o

I fall asleep pondering the proper form for a poem on
Borage. On waking, I have a song from musical thea-
tre – unheard and unconsidered, as far as I am aware,
for many years – on continuous mind-loop: a reminder
of the essentially anomic relation between the material
body and the eidetic formations of consciousness – a
factor which, in the composition of any text, constitutes
a significant limit to the illusion of formal mastery.

o

To imagine Borage is to isolate, from the endless enmeshment of thought and world, an eidetic object whose law of transformation and decay includes the action – albeit at some unmeasurable distance – of the actual, physical referent.

Thus, I will learn to consider Borage, in relation to its own text, as the agent of an inestimable yet mischievous causality.

o

In *De Rerum Natura*, the Epicurean poet Lucretius out-
lines a phenomenology in which all sensation is reduci-
ble to touch: 'For touch, so help me the holy power of the
Gods, it is touch that *is* the bodily sense.'

Every aesthetic experience, Lucretius tells us, can be
explained by the interactions of qualitatively diverse
atoms and their formations – of atoms subtle and coarse,
quick and lumbering, tangled and slippery, smooth or
hairy, hooked and combed: 'the liquids of honey and of
milk have a pleasant taste ... but wormwood and harsh
centaury twist up the mouth with a noisome flavour ...
those bodies which can touch our senses pleasantly are
made of smooth and round atoms, but contrariwise all
that seem to be bitter and rough are held in connection
by atoms ... accustomed to tear open their way into our
senses, to break the texture by their intrusion.'

Despite the ontological primacy given to the atom and
its motions in the Epicurean theorisation of the world's
becoming, this moment of the poem, which simply
assumes the existence of a percipient subject, intimates
a vertiginous reversal of explanatory priority in the text.
There emerges, here, a shadow Epicurus for whom it is
not the atoms which produce sensation, but sensation
– touch – which necessitates the analogical projection
of world in its material entity. For this Epicurus, the

theory of atoms is no more than an attempt to account for the mystery of those textural sensations in which we suddenly intuit ourselves as profoundly alien to the logic of the visibly extended and materially discrete – in which the world, strangely, is made flesh.

o

According to the herbalists, there is a febrifuge touch
of Borage; there is, too, a demulcent touch, a mucilagi-
nous touch, an expectorant, a sudorific and an emollient
touch.

○

There is a touch, I would add, whose teaching is the phenomenology of joy without reason.

o

According to prevailing philological wisdom, the texts
of Lucretius would have been unavailable to Dante.
Nevertheless, Dante's references to Epicureanism are
well known and despite philological objections, we can
imagine parallels between celebrated Dantean tropes and
images from Lucretius's poem. In *De Vulgari Eloquentia*,
his essay on vernacular poetics, Dante claims that words,
just as Lucretius's recombinant atoms, might be combed
and glossy, shaggy and bristly, liquid and yielding, and
goes to great lengths to define the mimetic logic of
language by matching these categorisations to specific
dialects, words, and even syllables. Indeed, it seems that,
in producing such a schema, Dante intended to establish
the possibility of a physics of permissible poetic form:
an investigation of the permutations and combinations
of syllabic atoms which would produce beautiful, rather
than monstrous poetic bodies.

The terms of this question, however, are complicated
by the imbrication of form and meaning at the heart of
every poem – for a form, Dante sees, will seem graceful
and appropriate only in proper relation to its matter. This
leads the poet into deeper meditation on how a poem's
sensuous aspects – the distribution of syllabic textures,
rhythm, rhyme, the economy of pauses – is related to its
content; a rich discussion structured by the intriguing
notion of an 'enlapment' (from the Latin *ingremiare* and

thus, really, 'enwombing') between form and meaning.

Through this notion, Dante seems to imagine an idealised, chiasmic entwining of sense and sensation in the formal unfolding of verse. Indeed, it is possible to imagine that, at the limit of this 'enwombing', Dante envisaged a miraculous poetic conception – a *coincidentia oppositorum* – in which content would be mysteriously one with the intricate textures of the sensuous word.

From the Epicurean sense of text as texture, we arrive at the mimetic embrace of a more-than-mortal world: the hope that an ultimate reality will descend from its otherworldly abstraction towards the flesh of feeling, and that this flesh will be raised into sense – the touch which speaks profoundest truth.

o

Just as, in Lucretius, the action of invisible atoms seeds the diverse appearance of natural forms, so, for Dante, the Garden of Eden, hidden from mortal sight at the top of Mount Purgatory, acts as the repository of an enigmatic germplasm – a bank of seed, scattered by zephyrs to the remotest earth. For Dante, then, it would be true to say that the origin of Borage is a wind which blows from paradise.

o

To happen on Green Hound's-Tongue: to be surprised
by leaves which, smooth and bright as those of early
beech, seem to foreswear the essential bristliness of the
Borages. But there is the special pleasure of that delicate
white down, super-subtle gossamer, which embraces
the nodding, plaited flower clusters of these plants –
closely woven stuff which conjures, for those who pass,
an impression of the ghost of blue; of a blue which has
recently fled, as when, on late-summer evenings, the sky
yields to a cooling exhalation of mist, the indrawn breath
of dusk.

o

To speak is not just to transmit meaning, but to affect oneself through the lingual pleasure of shaped and sounded breath. All speech yields to some degree, to a recursive, stimulant intention exceeding the practical. The semiotic: a diverting inward foliation lining language with touch.

o

The gentlest summer air is turbulent with fantastical
atoms – with the airy, intricate architectures of pollen;
with pollen polylobate, piliated, pstilate; perfectly round
and reticulated pollen; pollen pitted, scrunched inward
like sea-shell pasta; pollen annular and clavate, mono-
sulcate, rugose; pollen smooth above, yet, with spinula,
lavishly mulleted beneath; light or lumbering pollen;
thousands of windborne microscopic sponges, reefs of
pollen, in a coralline, invisible sea.

Like Cyclamen or the Bittersweet Nightshade, Borage,
with its reflexed petals, the oil-dark prominence of its
staminal cone, is a prototypical example of the flower
structure known to botanists as a 'shooting star'.
Through highly specialised interactions with bees, such
flowers are capable of copious ejections of dried, elec-
trostatic grains of pollen. A foraging bee will clasp the
Borage anthers in his pelted forelegs, yielding to a wild
thoracic vibration. Tuned to a deep co-evolutionary
frequency, the resulting resonance elicits, from the plant,
a spurt of fertile matter – a loop of futures, rich with
repetition.

o

The ability to succumb to a tactile resonance, a muscular hum directed from the wing attachment and enabling communication through body temperature, transmitted touch, is essential to the poetic eusociality of bees: a waggling bee on the surface of a swarm, for example, can communicate the direction and distance of a prospective nest-site; the same swarm, clustered with a hybrid intensity, can regulate its temperature through coordinated shuddering, and use this as a signal for collective departure.

For the bee, then, an individual Borage plant can be considered nothing but a single, luminous fold in a bright and poly-textural inwardness – a continuous membrane of significant vibrations – a music or prosody! – co-extensive with its own body.

○

This same world, the deep molecular magic of touch, exists in every pre-reflective action we perform: the motion of the fingers over the keys as I type, the unconscious adjustments of my big toe, gripping the textured carpet for balance as I walk. It is assimilated, ideally, to the performance of every delicate, specialised action – sporting, musical, artistic. It is focused in fingertips, in tongue and lips.

It is just this nervous, animal immediacy, moreover, which provides the only possible material analogy for that angelic, innocently pan-erotic communicative medium imagined by Dante; a language incarnate with sense.

o

An essayistic form seems most appropriate to the vegetable. For the essay expands, not because it advances towards some clearly defined limit, but on account of a habit of expressive involution – a turning back which would rescue every nuance, no matter how nugatory, from the oblivion of argument. The same is true of the growth of plants, a process for which every establishment of fixity – a flowering stalk, a leaf-stem, a shallow root – simultaneously defines a site of interstitial emergence, a betweenness charged with potential.

o

Green Alkanet, invader of cracked concrete, the angles of walls: spontaneous life which will not be paved over.

○

In the metaphysics of Leibniz, every event of sensation is, in potential, a book from which the whole universe might be deciphered: 'every body feels the effect of all that takes place in the universe, so that he who sees all might read in each what is happening everywhere, and even what has happened or shall happen ... But a soul can read in itself only what is distinctly represented in it. It cannot all at once unroll everything that is enfolded in it, for these things reach into the infinite.'

This is true, Leibniz says, because the universe is a 'plenum' – it contains no gaps. And so the basis of this startling vision of knowledge is the universal tangency of what is – a pantheistic touch.

o

I want a poem vivid with this linguistic yearning: the
desire to relate to the world, and to its own language, in
the manner of the illimitably extended body of touch –
the preconscious body which, caressing a leaf of Borage,
registers the minute and individual sensation of each
single hair; which, in the stubble field at night, separates,
from the swelling sound of beginning rain, the dash and
dot of each discrete and distinctive droplet; which hears
the rustle and reach of each wingtip's flex in the susurra-
tion of startled starlings.

o

The eye of touch is Borage blue.

II

PARASITE

Catching light in the glade, Robin's Pincushion I pinch
from Dog Rose: a gall wasp's nursery

At its base, folded in the navel, a sliver of leaf – its matter
and principle

With a chemical injection, the wasp deranges cell growth
in the leaf-bud

The gall exploits the plasticity of vegetable life, its
inexhaustible expression of foliar form

Is a scribble of the eternal leaf

Detached from its natural place, it looks a lost thing,
loosed from a forgotten pocket: tangle of strands, forked
with potential growth, its yellowish bigarrure shades
to a deepening heart-red – reflective, but tending to
absorption in the interior, to the chamber where the
larvae couch

In the rose's dentate leaf, growth moves from the planar
occupation of space towards the articulacy of line – each
angle, at the edge, might be drawn to the filament it
insinuates

Until, when the plant flowers, this formal process enters
a shift in phase – sublimation to the subtle, sculpted
surface of blossom, the expression of colour

So, successive impulses in the plant's development,
simultaneously hyper-realised, are the form of this
Pincushion

I place it, almost weightless, on my palm

Arc my fingers out and back, stretching the contact skin
to a smooth, sensitive surface

In the make of things, there are complement textures:
receptivity, here, rests in an act of formal opposition –
the medium made apt to its object

I walk onwards into shade with it placed there, arm
outstretched, a suppliant to the beech grove

A tingle of warmth and animation spreads to my palm,
outwards, in movement to occasion, and from out, in, to
a fix in proprioception – habitual motion, tempered to a
point of feeling stillness

In contemplation motion is a form of ease – as for the
gliding fulmar, hammocked in wind

Appropriated to life, we are drawn out into mystery,
must cleave to what unfurls in attention

So, to walk – which is to think – and write: the
successive cadence held as one

Picked by this Pincushion

○

beguiling eyes
a fly's
tachykinetic footfall
implies

a world

spliced
between times

○

WINDOW WITH REDWOOD

I

Because this window has been treated to reduce glare, I look right into the sunlight amongst the needles of the ornamental redwood.

Seeing them bristle with brightness, as if tense with an insubstantial presence, I am reminded of how in a long-ago classroom we children, playing with magnets, delighted in the swift and sensitive motions of iron filings.

I remember the tidal scratch of their shifts across paper, the sigh of a force finely feeling its body.

The recollection, though vivid, has neither measurable duration nor location; it is a circle of circumscribed vision, surrounded, as if seen through a microscope, with darkness, the idea of a sound.

To both aspects of this uncertain memory, the visual and the auditory, an intellectualised affect is appended, like the sadness, not truly sadness, summoned by a tragic play.

The affect attached to the sound-idea has a more realistic and possible presence; it could be accurately reanimated if I were to scratch the cheap electrostatic surface of the carpet with my fingernails.

The memory, then, is as a citation adequated to my current impressions; its sudden appearance confirms the power of reverie to summon the illuminating image: to construct a rebus of lived time, of a chronology which cannot be contained by a linear model.

II

What I see, beyond the window, is separate from what I hear inside the room.

The window, for this reason, could serve as an analogy for the divided nature of poetic language: for the ambiguous interactions between the images projected by words and the feelings associated with their imagined sounds, with the breathings and intervallic accents, the direction and destiny, of each carefully measured phrase.

What I see is a play of bright silence and light; what I hear is the small friction of feet, the patter of fingers on computer keys, the rustle of clothing.

Out there, soundlessly, the outer needles of the redwood caress the mossy sloping roof of a long, low building.

Opposite, an oak extends in sympathetic symmetry, its few last leaves luminous amongst the dark outlines of the boughs – as if each were the promise of one more bright winter sunset, a jewel in these days of rain.

Often, in my work, the window, with its restricted view, serves as a reminder of the limits to the free development and expression of life.

Such limits are an effect of the social metabolism, governed by its law of value: that, under unequal conditions, to work for money is the dominant mode of access to what keeps and grows life; that what is consumed is produced by the labour of others; that the circulations of these indirect, imbricated and international relations, like the growth rings of a tree, accumulate as our human geography – objectified historical time: this room, this window, the ornamental redwood.

III

Just as we are, so the redwood, which is two redwoods.

An alien redwood, lost in its English lawn; another redwood, which is the same redwood, living, lonely and open in an elemental world.

○

gift
of the Palearctic winds

a few flown fieldfare
staggered in blackthorn

the increments in their places

○

FALLEN BEECH

Each winter I'm drawn to it, this basalt-black horizon
in the wood.

Long and level, from the chaos of its blown-open pedestal,
shards of shattered heartwood,

twin trunks lie. A tome left open on its spine.
Along each damp cold length

surprising, delicate abstractions grow, have grown –
a frieze of tiniest fungi:

there is this smudge, bubbled and uncannily pink;
a daub of sloe-must blue brilliance;

here, porcelain arcs of clustered emergence hide
their intricate fan-vault gills; and

slung from spider-silk mycelium, like little balloons
buoyant in a world turned upside down

these several matchhead bunches of colour,
toyish and vulnerable.

Each seems a miracle of singularity, each
an unlikely, unrecoverable beauty.

Only a painter, maddened with skill, might hope to match
such fine formations of decay.

Striving to show them, my words – curling, indwelt
to the tongue's tangent palette –

would break off into babble, or unravel, held to the swift
asemic glide of the pen

the touch of it, recursive in the holding hand.
So, as migrant thrushes clatter

into mystic coverts, there is this pact with all that flies
from fixing look, from unincisive name.

○

through woods in winter

subtle colour
weaves its catachreses

○

ORGANON

There is a range of feelings experienced in the presence of natural events.

Amongst these our 'sense of natural beauty.'

I imagine this affect as a remnant of past potentiality; a swerve, untaken, in the history of what we recognise as proper to our species: thus, as the record of a relict, yet always latent, organ.

So that a plant or animal creature, for which we feel an unexpected love, could have been, to the invisible life of sense – the self given to itself – as, in the field of biological fact, mitochondria are to each single, animal cell.

To make such an intuition show itself, we assume these approximations, which we call concepts.

We work their internal, inherited differences, so they return to that future which was grasped, also, in them; their unity with the pre-intuited real.

So that, ideally, the progression of sentences in what is finally the poem will have the rhythmic working of the lived event it points to: exposure to a truth known in the time it will have already created.

In other words, the poem, once found, will have had, all along, the status of pre-appearance within the field of broader, yet unrealised possibility in what we are.

Will be, thus, the totem creature of its own emergence.

So that the whole of its speech can be considered a transliteration.

Through the field of phonemic happening of 'ordinary' language, the poem brings the imagined voice of that imaginary creature which it is.

○

I had sought
              a pathology
for my joy in spring

but these jade weightless openings
of whitebeam

○

Lightning Source UK Ltd.
Milton Keynes UK
UKHW021531300621
386361UK00006B/243

9 781999 971885